Susan Coventry

ODES TO NIGHTINGALES

for my surgeon

Odes to Nightingales

by

Susan Coventry

BEAUCLERK

PUBLISHING

British Library Cataloguing in Publication Data
A catalogue record for this book is available from the British Library

ISBN 0-9516505-3-X

Typeset by Amolibros, Watchet, Somerset
This book production has been managed by Amolibros
Printed and bound by T J International Ltd, Padstow, Cornwall

CONTENTS

PRELIMINARY TRAINING SCHOOL

INTO ST THOMAS'S HOSPITAL

In The Wards

Into The Night

Final Sketches

Cover sketch by kind permission of the Friends of St Thomas's
Hospital

ABOUT THE AUTHOR

Susan Coventry was born in 1932 at Alverstoke, Hampshire. She was educated at Moira House School, Eastbourne and trained to be a nurse in the Nightingale Training School at St Thomas's Hospital 1951-1955. Subsequently she became a child photographer till her marriage. In 1990 her first book about the Nightingale Training School, *Images of a Nightingale*, was published.

By the Same Author

Images of a Nightingale

Preface

Since my first book about my experiences in the Nightingale Training School for nurses at St Thomas's Hospital, was published in 1990, the School has closed. As a result, no more nurses will ever become Nightingales. We are a dying breed. This book, written in poetry, is our swansong. It looks back to the heyday of the Nightingale Training in the middle of the last century. Much of the contents have been taken from anecdotes recounted to me by other Nightingales, or written to me when my first book, Images of a Nightingale, came out. I have thus given it the title *Odes to Nightingales*.

LOYALTY,

HONOUR

AND

FORTITUDE

THE PRELIMINARY TRAINING SCHOOL

The First Ten Weeks

There was a special programme
To teach us all they could
In ten short weeks.
It was intensive and defensive
In its policy – in its mood.
We learnt about bones and blood
And veins and glands and physiology.
We improved apology.
We ran the whole gamut of hygiene and how to clean.
We learnt the fundamentals of nursing care,
And how to make a bandage,
Put it on and make it preen.
We crammed our latent brains to pass the tests
Written or viva all that time.
We were in our prime.

BUILDING A NIGHTINGALE
BRICKS AND MORTAR

To learn to be a Nightingale, we found
Discipline was built up from the ground.
To learn to be a Nightingale, were taught
Detail in every action taken, thought.
To learn to be a Nightingale, the real test,
We could not compromise, go for second best.

These rudiments we learnt at PTS,
As well as work that glimpsed the pending stress,
The confidence so easily broken,
The worm of guilt that could not be spoken.
The ease of failure, the unexpected ruts,
To ride all this, above all to have guts.

The Arrival
at the Manor House, Godalming

Arrived like roses,
Sat around,
Fifty girls with dewy faces.
Powdered noses,
Not a sound,
Whispered words as carried cases.

Tudor mansion
On a hill,
Fifty girls shown up to bedrooms.
In our fashion
Silent still,
Entered them with meek decorum.

Words began to crack
The surface,
Fifty girls became a Set.
Now a pack
We integrated
With forty-nine good friends we met.

Dressing for the Job
Seventeen Garments

You had a bra,
A vest or two,
Some thick, some thin,
Some white, some blue
That went down to
Beyond your crotch
With ribbon straps
You had to clutch
To stop them jumping
Down your shoulder
Or breaking on
The bosom boulder.

Elastic girdle
Next you wore,
From waist to buttocks
It would score
Deep furrows in
Your youthful flesh,
Your thighs compounded,
Stomachs crushed.
Suspenders held
The stockings' crown
To keep them up,
The girdle down.

Pants came next.
Two pairs were normal,
One as lining,
One more formal.

Then petticoats
With lacy trims,
More straps to hoick,
More laundry flims,
More pipes bedecked
With soaking clothes,
More steam inhaled,
More angry prose.

Then finally
The uniform.
Eight bits of it
To deck your form.
Then grips and pins,
Then laces, studs,
You pulled and pushed
With squeaks and thuds.
You reached around
To front reverse,
Until, at last,
You looked a nurse.

Anatomy and Physiology

I felt...
Anatomy was very hard work,
Physiology was fun.
Anatomy meant hundreds of names,
Physiology meant some.
Anatomy was like a steeple,
Physiology was like a junction,
Anatomy was about people
But not about their function.

JUST THE BONES

Your bones are laced together beads,
Head nodding like a mandarins.
Your beauty withered with our flesh,
Your sinews gone to dust and ash.
The rushing blood that gave you life
Has long since entered paradise.
Your ribs are spare, they have no heart,
No lungs to bare, or to be part.
Your pelvis is an empty grate,
Has lost its glands, its lust, its ache.
Your feet are cold from lack of socks,
One cannot rub their bony locks.
Oh skeleton, how sad you are
Without the breath that gave you fire.

LECTURES ON NURSING

Lectures on nursing,
We were rehearsing
What we would do
When we started on wards.

Could not imagine
The real McCoy in
Practice not theory
And nursing in hordes.

Listened with pleasure
To tutoring treasure,
Were just outsiders
Until were on board.

Anticipation
No close relation
To reality that
Experience affords.

High Jean

Lectures on hygiene started as a hit.
What? A million microbes to an armpit?
Germs world over, flood their venomous spore,
Count a billion on one square yard of floor.
Intestines are their richest breeding ground,
Some good, some bad, some dead, some hare, some hound.
One graze and bacteria begins a war,
Attack like maniacs on a broken pore.
It seemed germs were not a laughing matter.
It all became listen, not more natter.

So hygiene was about cleanliness, not laughter,
No mice should be swinging from the rafter,
No furry coats warming the Gloucester cheeses,
No weevils in the flour, no lice, no fleas.
It was about glistening sheets out on the line,
Surfaces free of dust, not a speck of grime.
About cleaning until your arms and back ache,
So much to worry you, so much at stake.
In a hospital multiply all this by four
To stop infection stampeding through the ward.

ALL-ROUNDERS

We learnt to sew and make a bandage
We learnt to be all-rounders,
We could fix a sling around a shoulder
Cook eggs and quarter pounders.
We had medicals to check our health
And BCGs protect us,
We learnt the art of saying "yes"
In fact the whole prospectus!

INTO ST THOMAS'S HOSPITAL

Limbering up in Lambeth

Not so bad a place. Not so bad.
Went out mostly woollen clad.
Liked the views around – the water flusters,
The skimming bridges and the temple clusters.
Liked the barges slung up one to t'other,
Linked together arm in arm each brother.
Always liked the red splayed mornings on the tide
Sweeping over houses from the eastern side.
Liked the air thrown from the Thames when breathing,
Fresh as peppermint and fishy seething.
Went for walks along the grey Embankment,
Locked in history's side by side encampment.
Liked the space that rushed from every angle,
No traffic jams there then, no nasty tangle.
In some hollow undetected spaces,
Little pubs were found and showed their graces.
Softer, smaller, less congested was the area,
Not so much a cosmopolitan interior.
Not so bad a place. Not so bad.
Let's be grateful to our heavenly Dad.

THE NIGHTINGALE PROBATIONER

In those old days we started
Mystified and meek,
Probationers warm-hearted,
Bottom of the heap.

Rather plainly clothed in
Purple white striped dresses
With starchy collar trusses.
Round our waists were stiff
Belts neatly studded.
We rubbed our shoes with polish
To shine about our feet.
Our stockings, like our shoes,
Were black and had the knack
Of breaking into ladders
Like stealthy, creeping adders.
To save five shillings more
Our fingers sewed and sewed
Along the cobble core.
Our caps were neatly drawn
On double cotton threads
That crowned our well groomed heads.
We wrapped ourselves in cloaks
And fixed the blood red yokes
Across the rounded mounds
That were our pounding chests
Inside thick layers of vests.

From PTS and theory
Then into the practice,
Nurses without axis
Or experience.
We were tumbled into
Routine tightened days,
Sister strictness ways
And conundrum maize.
Tried to feel out way through
Elementary fogs and

Comprehension bogs.
Hours of grimy dusting,
Hands made rough with scrubbing.
Folded gauze and dressings,
Knelt for prayers and blessings,
Reported to our seniors
Standing at attention.
Sisters rap and thunder
Often made us wonder
Why one was a nurse.
Tiredness wracked our beings,
Doubts and questioned fleeings.

Sharp initiation
Brought us to our senses,
Learnt the nursing tenses,
Confidence foundation.
Sister after sister
Drilled our minds and matter,
Stilled our idle chatter,
Planned our nursing bedrock
Through instruction methods
And masterly example
In that nursing temple.
So we held our heads up,
Stripped and made the beds up,
Learnt the vital lessons
In the vital ways.
When a year had passed, if
Somehow we had lasted
Were elevated up to
Staff nurse that was weathered.
Fledgling nicely feathered.

In those old days we started
Mystified and meek,
In one year solid-hearted
Branded with their teak.

The Downstairs Corridor

A quarter mile or more of belting length,
Few idlers here,
On whipping feet that skimmed the solid surface
Of the hard stone layer.

Destinations leapt from both its fractured sides
That drew us in,
To field a letter, mount a stair, to eat,
To learn our sins.

The concertina gates of lifts that crashed apart
For patients' beds,
The little men that pushed them straight in front
With rigid heads.

The boom of male throats that filled the walls
In echoes broken,
The nursing staff with flashing black-dressed legs,
Words hardly spoken.

The navy, red-lined cloaks that wrapped them round
In winter days,
Made spats of colour 'gainst the muddy yellows
And the middle greys.

To the dining room and City Ward and other
Destinations,
The central artery of the hospital
And its stations.

Visiting Matron's Office
Corridor and Rooms

Hushed as you walk the length,
Glistening and squeaky clean,
Shoes on the boards and strength
Cannot mark the sheen.

Walk through monastic air,
Silent in its womb,
Reaching that special layer,
Assistant matron's room.

Softly you tap the door,
Echoes sound and spin,
Knife of the voice in store
Invites you to come in.

Holy you go and stand
By the desk's attention,
Back used as lock for hands
And chin under detention.

Fear weighs your fragile choice
If you ask a favour,
Too early to rejoice,
Know if she will waver.

Worse if you've made a blob
On hospital's cantation,
Eyes looping over specs
Give an admonition.

Under the mask you see,
As time there crawls and creeps,
Beads of humanity
Coming from her lips.

THE BLESSED DINING ROOM

Great big tables, smooth and brown,
Hunched up nurses curling down,
Giggles bouncing in the air,
Intrigue burrowed in your care.
Gossip, gossip, gossip trite,
Freedom in your spade of light.

Oh the joy of sitting down
In your gracious, spacious ground.
Outwards gushed our ward-time sores,
Cradled in this nest of yours.
Had it not been for your sheath
Nurses might have sunk beneath!

Windows threw light round your walls,
Views of boats, their sounds and calls.
Juggly water, seagulls crying,
We forgot the dead and dying.
Replenished in your hall of balm
Spirits flew away from harm.

Dining room we will remember
Till the day has burnt its ember,
Bursts of energy you gave us,
All the subtle morale favours
To those embryonic girls
Learning life in nursing thralls.

A Song to Canteen Food
Circa 1950-1960

In the fifties it was over boil
And braise and mash and strain,
It was gravies thick as fossil fuel,
The vegetables were slain.
It was liver hard as granite rock
And top rump full of gristle,
With blood that oozed and jellified
Against the sausage missile.

You ate your stews with multi veg,
You ate your Shepherd's Stye,
You ate your rissoles scrag end bits,
You ate the curried pie,
You ate the dried eggs scrambled up,
Old boiled eggs taste of sulphur,
You never said a word about
The bone that caused an ulcer.

The puddings, too, were standard fare,
Like sago, tapioca,
Rice pudding with its burnt brown skin
And Spotted Dick – a choker.
Custard always there to give
Each pudding yellow uppers,
With fruits and prunes and jellies too
It covered all the suppers.

Those were the days of eating up,
The days of not complaining,
You made the most of every cup
Of soup that needed straining.
The tepid bits that should be hot,
The rest that should be cold,
It was a world of shutting up
And doing what you were told.

BIG BENJAMIN

Big Ben was the central spine of our punctuality,
Striking like a colossus, it refracted our personality.

One strike and we whipped from the dining room floor,
Two...were hurtling along the downstairs corridor,
Three...would arrive at the bottom of the stairs,
Four...in the ward in time for prayers.
Five...ready reporting at sister's desk,
Six...our schedule had been expressed.
Seven...halfway through the evening rush.
Eight...had washed those needing a wash.
Nine...made the beds, running towards the deadline.
Ten...coped with visitors, pushing them out in time.
Eleven...patients drugged and tucked up for the night.
Twelve...turned out each patient's light.

Not quite that speed – not quite the order or ingredients
But how that clock, that massive clock, demanded our obedience.

In the Wards

The Traditional Nightingale Ward

Deep-hearted and one hundred foot and plus in length,
Traditional wards stretched and stretched out dour strength.
Air breathed round their thirty patients on three sides
From windows high and bright, and luminous and wide.
Two strips of fifteen beds with central gully.
Filled with pillars, desk, sterilisers, trolleys.
Each patient seen from any, every angle view,
No need for bells to call us in their ceaseless mew.
A waving arm and attention straight was given,
The ward contained it all for quick revision.
Total orderliness central to the ward's good prep,
Its jutting beds in perfect symmetry and step.

Long, high, wide were St Thomas's ward dimensions.
Fundamental core of the Nightingale tradition.

THE HONOURED GUEST

Florence Nightingale said,
"Every patient should be
Treated as an honoured guest."
That was her behest,
The backbone of our training,
The caring and explaining.

We nursed them with our hearts,
We nursed them with our eyes,
Every one befriended
That we cared for, tended.
We never did refuse,
In any way abuse
The Nightingale creed
In their every need,
Her standards were the crest,
Our training was its quest
For youth and duty then.
In no way could we fail
To be a Nightingale,
Nor would we have preferred
To be a lesser bird.

As a Nightingale

As a Nightingale you learnt
To stretch the minutes out
Like pastry on a board.
The more you rolled,
The more you found
To fill with duty fillings
The A to Z of daily round.

As a Nightingale you learnt
The triplication of time
By juggling seconds.
To feel guilt at sitting down
Hands empty or unemployed.
You learnt to work drown.

As a Nightingale you learnt
That fatigue is just a syndrome:
That body time has become a clock
With automatic chime.

Five Nightingale Sisters

Sister City was a doll,
Dressed so carefully in her clothes
That smoothed and patted round her hips,
Voice tuttering out of china lips.
Her temper striking matches rose
From swinging heels and flaring nose.
A total contrast when she jested,
Her body shapely, heavy breasted.
She loved the doctors and she fluttered,
She was a sort of doctor's moll.

Sister Christian was a panther,
A dark and smooth and rapid mover.
Her eyes and hair were like burnt toast,
Could move things round like poltergeists.
She pounced upon her nurses folly,
Galvanising half-wit wallys.
But with the patients was so calm,
A blanket bath ambrosial balm.
She loved her patients like a litter,
This clever wit and easy ranter.

Sister Arthur was a card,
And born to nurse the better men.
Policemen loved her jolly railing,
Wisdom soft on human failing.
Was good with patients, good with staff,
Had a bass rotating laugh.
Her impact came with patients dying,
Rallied nurses, sent them flying.
Legs were stiff as flag posts leaning,
Walked quite fast and was low-browed.

Sister Beatrice was a mask,
Austere, contained with moon high standards,
Not a flick of light got through
Her moulded features straight at you.
Even when she gave a row
Addressed your cap, addressed your brow.
Held her specs case in both hands,
Waving them when taking stands
Or making points of emphasis.
A genius at her every task.

Sister Nuffield was a bird,
Tiny in her build and shape,
Not a cell of her was spared,
With laser movements worked and cared.
She did not suffer fools it seems,
And spoke her mind in reams and reams.
Intolerant with patients too,
But nursed them all ways through and through.
Many feared small Norah Nuff,
But learnt their stuff on wings and word.

SISTER NUFFIELD PROCLAIMS

Six probationers standing in a row,
All of them useless, they should know.
Compared with the Orderly, none of them stood
The ghost of a chance to be any good.

SISTER CHRISTIAN STATES

"What are you doing, nurse, where are you going?"
"I'm rolling some bandages just for the moment."
"Come now and help me with Mrs Brown's bed,
Her linen is dirty, her dressing had leaked,
The dressing is done, so quickly the bed,
Bring over the trolley and don't hang your head."

"What are you doing, nurse, where are you going?"
"Replace Miss Leak's catheter, was overflowing."
"Do it now quickly and don't stand and frown,
Mr Boggon's expected and screens must be down.
Then set a lumbar puncture for Mrs Spine,
As quickly as possible, gracious don't whine."

"What are you doing, nurse, where are you going?"
"To change Mrs Dribble's sheets and drawsheet,
She wanted a bedpan but wasn't in time,
She's been quite incontinent, wasn't her fault."
"Leave it to me, nurse, and just go to lunch,
Next time, for heaven's sake, show me more punch."

"What are you doing, nurse, where are you going?"
"I was just thinking what's best to do next."
"Thinking, nurse, *thinking*, good gracious stop that,
Never think when you better can act.
You and the others are here for the sick,
Go and look after them, don't be so slack."

Do Not Answer Back

Do not answer back,
Rig your mental tack,
You are on the rack,
In for Sister's flak,

If you do not hide
Choppiness inside.
Arguments and pride
Learn to law abide.

Arrow held in bow,
Do not let it go,
Heartache must not show,
Dam its pressing flow.

Never were you bold
In those days of old,
Poured inside a mould
Obedience was pure gold.

Home Thoughts About Abroad
1949

Sister Beatrice, Sister Nuffield, Sister Christian drove to France...
Some Nightingales sat down and thought, perhaps there was a
    chance...
A broken shaft...a tyre that burst...a brake that went...a wheel too
    slack...
But two weeks later, this frightening trio, in perfect order, all came
    back!

CITY OF LONDON WARD

Men's casualty – dear City,
You seemed a little smaller than he rest.
Not so. You too had thirty beds,
Winged outhouses, a straight but mini corridor,
Your special character, your *savoir faire* and law.

What memories – dear City,
The warming summer fanning the verandah,
The beds pushed out along the Thames,
The cockney vowels that split the unsuspecting ear,
The broken legs yanked high up in the air.

Your old gaffers – dear City,
With home-rolled cigarettes in yellow teeth,
Or toothless gums in hollow mouths
Propped up against the pillows or sunk into the beds,
The bulk of bedclothes severing the small grey heads.

The crisis moment – dear City,
The trolleys gushing in from Casualty,
The blue screens hastily arisen:
The strutting and swishing of the specialist:
The murmuring: the frantic relative who kissed.

You are gone now, City, you are gone,
As has your Sister with her blush and snap.
With shut eyes, the image is entire,
The geometry of all the orthopaedic strap,
And Sister's heels that filled the floors and walls with tap.

ELIZABETH
EYE WARD

Patches in snatches along the ward stretches,
Puppets of patients their bandages fresh,
Dressings that garnish the delicate tissues,
The itchy small stitches that knit up the flesh.

Careful and fearful of damaging op sites,
Of managing patients too quickly, too much,
Heads held up stiff against chimneys of pillows,
Movements so gentle, so rigid, no rush.

Turning and learning the critical nursing,
Standing them, landing them without a slew,
Unwrapping the strapping in circular movements,
Inspecting the swelling, the oozing, the glue.

Wiping the eyelids so lightly when swabbing,
Never too tightly when bandaging back.
Patients so patient, so stationed so long for
Not to disturb all the mending and pack.

New Probationer
Opening out in Alexandra Ward

I had never heard
The word
Colostomy.
But later was taught
Ostomy meant opening into.
But that was later.
Like a fish's mouth
It stared at me
And I stared back.
I wondered which of us
Would be the first to crack.

Not Washing a Patient
in Clayton Ward

I nursed a man who said to me
"Just wash my face and hands
Because the night nurse does it all,
The nooks and crannies
Everything – don't worry nurse
I'm washed you know,
From top to toe,
Just do my face and hands."

To night nurse he had said the same.
"Just wash my face and hands
Because the day nurse did it all,
The nooks and crannies
Everything – don't worry nurse
I'm washed you know,
From top to toe,
Just do my face and hands."

So Mr Blake was never washed,
He stayed a dirty grey
'Cos the day nurse thought the night nurse washed,
The night nurse thought the day.

REVOLUTION IN EDWARD WARD

A Jewish patient said
He would not lie in bed
Beneath a counterpane
That bore a Christian stain.

He shook his Jewish crown
When Sister sent him down
The ward to try and hide
The naked blanket side.

The Jewish patient broke
The ward rules at a stroke.
He did not want a fuss
Nor die beneath the Cross.

A Death in America Ward

The little girl died at the end of the day,
Her head in the lap of her pillow's bouquet,
The sweat had gone from her shadow like brow,
The plug had been pulled on vitality now.
Her laughing eyes closed, her fingers were crossed,
The beautiful promise, the future was lost.
In the terrible ravage of disease and decay,
The little girl died at the end of the day.

The little girl lived just the morning before,
The embers of life still smouldering at four.
She was not, she said, frightened by her end or her loss,
The pain in her head made her tremble and toss.
The vanishing interest, the vanishing sight,
The senses dissembled, the slow losing fight.
Disease was winning its inexorable war,
The little girl lived just the morning before.

The little girl lived once again on the morrow,
The death of her shell had removed all her sorrow.
Her spirit was loose in a freedom and light,
It danced in ineffable joy and delight.
Her parents, her loved ones felt only this peace,
The shadows of suffering were lost without trace.
The pain had been something she'd just had to borrow,
The little girl lived once again on the morrow.

A Nightmare
About a Sunday Service in George Ward

A doctor at the door,
A bedpan spilt on floor,
Whimperings for attention,
Sterilisers in contention,
Canular block,
Drugs out of stock,
Relations pestering,
Wounds festering,
The inside telephone
A ceaseless invasion,
The outside one
Some dreaded occasion.
Prayers trying to be read,
One patient three-quarters dead.

Then I woke up, it was just a dream.
It did not happen at all.
For the Sunday service, all was peace.
Nothing dared go wrong at prayer time.
That was forbidden.

La Ronde

Mostly largish, tall and broad,
Hard held features, medium bored,
Four steps forward, one to side,
Face the patient, lift the notes,
Questions smooth and stiff white coats.

Turn down bedclothes, lift the gown,
Pummel tummy, slight creased frown,
"Does it hurt you? Not at all?"
Down the nightie, up the sheet,
Notes replaced and stop complete.

And so consultants did their rounds,
Guarded by their various hounds:
Registrars almost as grand;
Housemen anxious with the answers;
Sisters acting as the bouncers.

THREE HUNDRED POUNDS A YEAR
CIRCA 1950s

Transfusions, confusions, coats flying, masks sighing,
The stethoscope bulging, the scribbling of notes.
The dashes, the flashes, the paces, the races,
The houseman is coming who carries the totes.

The general factotum, the treadmill, the rota,
Struggling with veins that have gone off on strike,
Drawing off blood for a flood of inspections,
Passing the tubes from the nose to the dyke.

In for a crisis, a puncture and juncture,
In for a block in the canular head,
Troublesome patients who discharge themselves and
Informing consultants the latest one dead.

Never a moment from the dawn to the gloaming,
Does this man feel he is out of the gear,
A year under pressure, a few drops of leisure,
And a miserable sum of three hundred a year.

MEDICAL EGGS

Students, students everywhere,
Shy, bewildered, awkward, spare,
Trailing round in lumpy circles,
Staring at the patient's blank,
Scribbling notes on bony flank.

Students, students lolloped in
To those wards of fierce routine
Gilded with their sisters' spleen.
Students were so green and fresh,
Out of touch with bones and flesh.

Students, students low on flare
Hovering in a limbo layer.
Asking patients where they hurt,
Could they breathe? Was there hope?
Fumbling with the stethoscope.

Students, students moving round,
Baggy, saggy, laggy sound.
Poor old students, what a sell
To face so many well-trained nurses
Dab hands at medicinal verses.

Students, students like a swarm
Round consultant's queen bee form.
Safe in numbers in the fold,
Listening, trying hard to latch
Onto knowledge and to hatch.

Students, students everywhere
Nor any single wink.

SCREENING

Hump the screens,
Bump the screens,
And jolly well
Lump the screens.

Numbering Screens

One screen meant
A special patient
At the top of the ward,
Occasionally a specialist
With a student horde.

Two screens meant a wash,
A fresh dressing,
A doctor inspecting
The distressing.
A lumbar puncture
Or a catheter passed,
Enemas flurried soap
Or the bedpan fast,
A sudden crisis
The scramble that went,
A very sick person
In an oxygen tent.
A dying person
The relations sobbing,
A nurse holding the pulse
The diminishing throbbing.

But three screens meant
As certain as read,
A patient not dying
But a patient dead.

A Nurse Suffers Deeply

Your chopped up slow breathing, your sunken lid eye,
Oh patient, we did not want you to die.

We sat at your bedside, sweat wiping your brow,
Tight holding your hand in the terrible now.

Those stiff, broken words said close to our faces,
Moving along with you to those strange places.

Beloved, dear patient till your last sighing breath,
A nurse suffers deeply your dying and death.

FAHRENHEIT

Now in these days of centigrade,
The temperatures are in the shade.
How cold it is at thirty-six,
Ice in our veins, ice on our wicks.
How golden were the days of yore,
The days of ninety-eight point four.

High Dusting

Somewhere hidden up the wall
There lurks a veritable shawl
Of dust and smut that cling in heaps
Above where old Ma Tangmere sleeps.

You have a duster on a pole,
A wobbly, heavy toppéd roll
That slides along the ledge and nook
So high you break your neck to look.

Then in the air dust feathers flock
Instead of in the duster's tuck,
And fall on old Ma Tangmere's head
Or on the bottom of her bed.

In the Sluice

Freezing arctic hollow,
Chromium bedpan ware,
Rubber macs
Lie in stacks,
Dangling tubes confer.

Marbled fingers scrub
Sheets in water lime,
Brushes rub,
Brushes grub,
Lift off all the grime.

Sputum mugs bang their lugs,
Jostling on a tray.
Tow on wall,
In its stall,
Ready for foray.

Water in this quarter
Sloshed round sinks of stone.
Linen tubs,
Wheely hubs,
Centre of this drone.

Sluice turns nurses puce,
Little cotton dresses,
Time scales rush,
Time scales crush,
Cleaning all the messes.

New Probationer
Inside Out

Commode was lifted to the sluice,
Forgot the bowl came out,
I tripped and fell across its top,
The whole caboodle crashed to slop
Across the oak strip floor.

The ugliness inside us all,
The guts, the brains, the glands, the waste.
Everybody thin or stout,
The grace of God is beauty out.

BACKS

In attending to backs,
We could not be lax,
'Cos a bedsore was
A Nightingale cross.

WE WASHED YOUR FACE AND HANDS

When a trolley rolled from theatre with your case,
Tube jack hanging from your face as breathing brace,
When consciousness drew life back to your face,
We washed your face and hands.

When you vomited post-op or you were bilious;
Your fever settled rigour into stillness;
You spilled your food, exhausted by your illness;
We washed your face and hands.

Sometimes in the middle throat of deepest night,
Under petticoat blue cloths that veiled the light,
When waking up in wretchedness or fright,
We washed your face and hands.

When you snatched in breath with little snacks of air,
A breath that rattled, battled in despair,
When helpless, needing kindness or repair,
We washed your face and hands.

The Death of the Blanket Bath

Our days were full of blanket baths,
That special form of caring.
The intimacy that emerged
Between the patient and her nurse
When washed from this luxuriant base
Between the sheet and blanket space.

The kindliness that each one found
Where conversations were profound
When washing hands and breasts and backs
And powdering all the folds and cracks,
When wiping sweat and rubbing heals
By gentleness, through fingers feel
The throbbing pulse, the nightgown crease
That water, love, position ease.
A blanket bath broke up the strain,
Brought down the fever, eased the pain,
Because it was a tenderness,
Made good things better, bad things less.

And now that care has gone away,
The blanket bath does not exist,
There's no more time for all that love
And nursing moves down different paths.
Patients, however ill they are,
Are lowered into tepid baths.

Finishing Off the Blanket Bath
Men's Medical

"What do I 'ave to finish orf?
What do I 'ave to do, nurse?
You've done me all
That I can think.
I feel so clean
And nice and fresh.
Don't look at me so worried like,
Just tell me what I finish orf."

PILLOW CASE OPENINGS

When making a bed remember this law,
Pillow case openings must turn from the door.
Five pillows, six pillows, seven pillows, eight,
All must be facing the Thames in this state.

If pillows are vertical, openings go down,
To leave a neat top for the sister and rounds
And stop the dust dropping down into the casing.
Bound to this habit, a lifetime of placing.

The Abominable Abdominal

With blanket stitch you sewed the straps,
That crab-like bandage with its flaps,
In flannelette wrapped bodies round,
Just overlapping, each on each
As far as nurse could make it reach
To hold the dressing tight in place
And not to bring its nurse disgrace,
Who wrapped and wrapped and wrapped and pinned
It round the patient's abdomen.

THE WATER PILLOW
(ALIAS AIR RETENTION PILLOW)

Square of rubber,
Square of fear,
Try to fill me
If you dare.

I'm made to test
Your dedication,
Obedience
And subjugation.

I'm difficult
To fill with water
And I vomit
As I oughter.

When you squeeze me
On your laps
To ease out bubbles
From the flaps
That double up
Across my front
I gargle, chuckle,
Seem to grunt.

You hate me
With my nodding head,
I like to burst
When I'm in bed.

But sister loves me
'Cos I make,
Good comfort for
The patient's sake.

MICROBES

It was a mystery
In history,
Infection and why.
You could not see germs,
You could not hear them,
They multiplied spontaneously
Beyond the eye.

LYSOL

Lysol was a darkish bay
And shone like shampoo,
But when mixed with water
It was like white clouds
Billowing in a paper sky.
It made the germs die.

GERMAL INTERCEPTORS

The sterilisers were the masters,
So they thought,
They the central germal blasters,
We were taught.
Three minutes killed the common rascals,
Dead on time,
Twenty for the noble grafters
And the slime.
In that boiling, toiling water well,
We just hoped,
No microbe could survive the hell
Or was just doped.

The steam came belching, settling scores
Up our faces,
It bleached and braised our facial pores
At five paces,
It scorched our arms and skinned our jaws
If not careful,
And spat at us without a cause,
Gave an earful.
Ruffed up the smoking, curling air
From its bubbles,
It was not one, it was a pair,
So double troubles.

The catheters cruised round like snakes
In great numbers,
The rubber gloves blew up like bakes
And did rumbas,
The forceps crouched like furry rakes
On the bottom,
The porringers' limescale looked like flakes
Of something rotten.
All the rest were just a jumble
Of instrument jollies,
Waiting for a nurse to humble
When setting trolleys.

The Ward Routine

In those days ward routine moved like
A beautifully oiled bike.
Everyone knew which cog they were
And how and why and where.
Strata were never crossed,
More junior were more bossed.
Standing back from a distance
It might have appeared to have had
The choreography of a dance.
You fitted in where you should,
Never where you could.

THE DIFFICULT PATIENT
IN CITY WARD

"I'm burstin' for a bottle, nurse,
I'm longin' for a drink,
I 'aven't 'ad me tablets yet,
Nor slept a single wink.
Mr Barnard's coughed till mornin',
And I'm so much in pain.
What! Doctor says I'm goin' 'ome
And in a bloody train?"

Post Operational
In Nuffield Ward

The operation was completed,
Up and down his bed he slid,
Semi-conscious, moaning, wailing.
Nightingale went to his bedside,
"Did you call me Mr Kidd?"
"If your name is Christ,
I did."

PROFESSIONAL LOVE
IN ARTHUR WARD

You brush my heart
With shielded glances,
Flaps of hair
And molten charm.
But what chances
Have I there,
Disrupted calm
Or fever chart?

I lift you weightless,
Faces touch,
Your body softens
Straightened sheets.
Vibrations such
My breath is often
Drawn in pleats
Of tenderness.

But in this thrall
A nurse is held,
I tend your needs
With steadied mind.
Affections weld
With routine deeds,
My love is kind
It can but crawl.

Cardiac Arrest
In George Ward

He sat down with a graceful air,
His legs so loosely spread and spare.
Above his specs his golden eyes
Looked round the ward with scant surprise.
His pipe sucked in his youthful mouth
Sent rings of joy both north and south.
His paper folded down to columns
Gave his face its lifts and solemns.
A man complete for just a while,
A man beloved, a man with style.

But suddenly it all went flat,
The spare parts fell into his lap.
A crumpled man without expression,
Who'd lost control of all possession.
Each feature dropped its special frame
Related to the world by brain;
And nerves that could not move or tense
The feelings that had lost all sense.
The fearful power of that small organ
To rid a life of all dominion.

SENIOR STAFF NURSE

The higher you went,
The better it came,
It was less of a rush
And more of your brain.

We were respected
By more and more staff,
Once sisters rejected
Now suddenly laugh.

First only the whey,
Then merely the milk,
Now are the cream
And join with that ilk.

The doctors look at you
Not through an X-ray,
The patients attract you
As people and play.

There is time for discussion
And time to reflect,
The terror that struck you
You now can deflect.

You now have the keys
To important locked doors,
The drugs and the linen
Eventually yours.

No longer the witness,
No longer the slave,
Now *you* make decisions,
Certain, not brave.

INTO THE NIGHT

Night Duty

Living in the night
On a ward; empty of normal routine.
Empty but for three nurses
And a regiment of mostly silent patients
Restoring their unconscious strength.

Duty guided by your ears,
Your instinct, your touch.
You do your rounds in silent shoes.
You reach the sick through
The junction of nerve ends
And senses: care that's feather-soft.
The night like a black gown
Changes nursing into invisible
Communication, but profound.

THE DARKNESS HAS DROPPED

The darkness has dropped, darkness has fallen,
Over the hospital, into the Thames,
Darkness has dropped like a cloak in the wards,
Hushing its movements, hobbling its speed,
Darkness has fallen and broken its seed.

Lights in the wards are dressed up in blue,
Crouched is the centre light over the desk.
Cloths are sweltering over the sickness,
Uncannily staining the pallor of faces,
Night lights in blue drop down in places.

Whispering nurses creep on the ward wood,
A torch and a pen and a watch and a word.
Mrs Jane Young has asked for some water,
Old Mother Crane is banging her cylinder,
Whispering nurses move it away from her.

Darkness has fallen into the night
Increasing the sound of a switching of light;
A book on the floor like the crack of a whip;
A repetitive cough like the rasp of a horn.
With its own special varnish, darkness is born.

Sleep Walking through St Thomas's

Passages in night light veils,
Fragile moonbeams glancing through,
Echoes beating in the stairwells,
In the blackness, in the blue.

Wrap your cloak round frigid shoulders,
Run the gauntlet of the night,
Feel the vastness crush your smallness,
Feel the tendrils and the fright.

See the wan lights dripping wattage,
Speed beneath them all alone.
Hear the chopping of your footsteps
Wiping silence off the stone.

Matron's office yawning, hollow,
Queen Victoria's shadows drop
From the statue in the main hall
A cloak around her plinth and prop.

Look through windows cross the water,
Shaded temples up and down,
Till the orange of the morning
Burns the blackness into brown.

Leap the mounting stairways homeward,
Racing shadows by your side,
Heartbeats halfway through your breast straps,
Breath is caught on rising tide.

Then your ward is just ahead now,
Wooden floors on which you creep,
Warmth and kinship quickly swallow
Anxiousness in hives of sleep.

Night Sister's Round

Thump, thump, thump,
Your heart extra systolizing
Like an irregular pump,
Skipping about like a baby's.
Waiting for Night Sister,
Waiting for Night Sister,
Checking your notes.
A cool surface hides
A large internal lump.

Tap, tap, tap,
Her footsteps penetrate the stone.
You jump to your feet, snap,
Like an alert animal.
Night Sister has arrived,
Night Sister has arrived.
You walk with measured steps
To greet her at the door,
Ready for this intense lap.

Stop, stop, stop
At the bottom of each bed.
Details of each patient hop
Like insects round your head.
Night Sister is listening,
Night Sister is listening,
Never a slip must you make.
Sister has all the answers
Tucked away in her crop.

Time, time, time
Remembering all those names
In this mental climb.
No excuses, never any.
Night Sister knows,
Night Sister knows,
Every name in the block,
All the information you forgot
In this night round rhyme.

Early Morning in Lilian Ward

Seconds

Rushing, rushing,
Potties,
Washing, flushing,
Brushing,
Cots to make,
Specimens.
Lists to fill.
Everything that
Can will spill.

In a state,
One morning,
By a mistake,
Too late,
I fed one baby twice.
Was it sick in cot?
Did the other
Cry all morning
For its mother?

Sixteen Deaths in George Ward

Three months night duty in George,
Men's medical ward, top floor.
Cardiac cases, lungs, blood flaws–
Clotting in the veins, emulsifying–
Taking away sixteen good men
Of all ages. Lives nullifying.
And so they left us, heart wrench, heart sore.

Three months night duty in George.
Young nurses of twenty-one, mind bled
For all those men, suddenly dead.
Wept in our souls in duty rushes,
All our energy and discipline
With the last office that death hushes,
Bathing and wrapping the lives that fled.

EASY TO KNEEL AND PRAY

The night's claws are sheathed
By the stillness of silence,
By the softness of darkness,
By the pale, languid moon,
By ward beds draped in grey.
Easy to kneel and pray
In the night.

FINAL SKETCHES

IMAGES OF THE THEATRE

Images of green
Splashing red inside it.
Figures, fingers, wandering
Round its central orbit.
Gasping breathing bag,
Pulsing, rippling organs,
Organs moving, moving
Like an engine room,
Everything in sequence,
Bulging in their membranes.

Cut and tie and snip,
Suction for the blood streams,
Eye across meets eye,
Voices tie in harmony.
Questions, quick replies,
Prise and cauterise.
Wiping, wiping round,
Swabs lie on the ground,
Waiting to be shaken,
Waiting to be counted.

Now the final stitch,
Iodine is splashed,
Dressing then applied,
Scene disseminates.
Backs turned round on bodies.
Gloves are pulled off first,
Gowns and masks are thrown,
All appears disorder.
Porters inward rush
Blowing out the hush.

Breaking up the strain,
Bringing back the pain.

The Surgeon

The surgeon stumps, the surgeon roars,
He holds aloft his well scrubbed paws,
The wheel of theatre round him tours,
This thespian knows he gets applause,
Experience in his stature soars,
He has the height, the build, the jaws,
With confidence there is no pause,
He loves the job, he has good cause.

For in the coming operation,
He never looks below his station
Nor could this maestro share the label
With lesser mortals round the table.

POINTS ABOUT JOINTS

Pick up a pin?
Then bend your knees,
Back joints do not
Grow on trees.
Let joints in your arms
And legs take the weight,
The ones that get
Arthritis late.
But when you are young
It's backs that suffer
So use the others
As the buffers.
And when you are old
And hobbling about,
The arthritic joints
Can be taken out.

BLOCK

Once a year
With lecture gear
The nursing flock
Returned to Block.*

United in,
Excited in
The classroom bowers
Of chattering showers.

To listen to
The tutors' mew
Or doctors' rock
Our virgin stock.

Our leaky brains
Went under strains
To keep astride
The blackboard ride.

The sister Tutor
Was a rooter
Of her students'
Indolence.

Behind thick specs
Saw laggard lakes
Of those far back
To skirt the flak.

But memories pocked
Became well stocked
With all the guile
Of this wise owl.

The doctors boomed
About the room
The last advance
In medicine science.

Some sacred cows
Made exit bows,
While others came
To fill the frame.

"Now this drug here
Was banned last year,
The side effects
Could change your sex.

We've found one better
Than the latter,
Did discover
Could recover."

So did they fill
Our curious will,
To keep abreast
With theory's chest.

And stuff with shock
Our knowledge block,
And fill with thrills
Our learning tills.

*   St Thomas's Hospital lecture periods

Barbiturates

Amytal and Medinal
Cafinal and Didial
Heberal and Nembutal
Seconal and Soneryl
Luminal and Brominal
Allonal and Bellergal
All these drugs were dispensable,
Knocking many people insensible.

THE NIGHTINGALE COMPLETE

After years of chipping, we had been made a special stock,
The hard lines of training that sisters bevelled from each block.
We had known fear in most of its unwelcome guises,
The lashing tongue, the broken breath, the nasty surprises.
We had known fatigue where legs immobilised on the spot,
We had known achievement too, where a dash had grown from a dot.
We had grown from the simplest most innocent seed
Into people seamed together forever as a breed.

When Nightingales get together to reminisce and philosophise,
We know we work better under pressure, can improvise.
Always feel guilty resting, feel that we shouldn't,
Have the ability to cope with the exceptional, where once we couldn't,
Never feel self-pity, martyrdom or cup half-empty,
Always know that better times will come in their plenty.
We are observant, punctual perfectionists, *de rigueur*,
Stamped for life with the Nightingale insignia.

L'ENVOI

The end has come
For Nightingales
That sang in Lambeth's grubby vales.

With folden wing
And silent tongue,
Our years of usefulness are done.

The doors are closed,
The trees divest,
The last badge clipped to feathered breast.

So no more birds
Learn in the wards
The arts of healing and accord.